GW01403020

Reiki For Beginners

The Complete Guide to Mastering Reiki Healing to Reduce Stress

TABLE OF CONTENTS

Introduction

I want to thank you and congratulate you for downloading the book, *"Reiki for Beginners."*

This book contains proven steps and strategies on how to learn Reiki healing to reduce stress.

Reducing stress every day is vital at maintaining overall fitness as it could improve your disposition, boosts immunity, and promotes long and a more fruitful life. When you allow stress to get the finest in you, you place yourself in danger of acquiring a variety of ailments, which can take the form of a common flu to a severe cardiovascular disease.

Stress holds such an influential impact upon the well-being because it exists as an innate response that stays activated within the mind. So, what should you undertake to move yourself towards a better pattern, besides reducing stress? Among the highly effective, as well as rewarding, techniques remains Reiki healing.

Reiki, an art of recovery originating from Japan, is based upon the faith that all human beings carry a life or universal force. Like the mainstream of Eastern beliefs, the knowledge of Reiki captures an all-inclusive approach towards healing.

Thus, in place of swallowing a recommended pill three times daily, the exercise of Reiki encompasses the entire person, functioning to cure the brain, body, sentiments and soul all at the same time. By refining emotional conditions, promoting serene feeling, the exercise of Reiki could dramatically lessen stress.

There exist many dissimilar styles and elements of Reiki healing, though it usually works through the laying of the hands upon different places in the physique and in diverse combinations. Remember that Reiki requires the expert to maintain his fingers altogether towards properly guiding the universal power.

Therefore, you could reduce stress dramatically through Reiki by creating its exercise an everyday habit. And this book will show you how. Thanks again for downloading this book, I hope you enjoy it!

© **Copyright 2014 by Jonathan Brown - All rights reserved.**

This document is geared towards providing exact and reliable information in regards to the topic and issue covered. The publication is sold with the idea that the publisher is not required to render accounting, officially permitted, or otherwise, qualified services. If advice is necessary, legal or professional, a practiced individual in the profession should be ordered.

- From a Declaration of Principles which was accepted and approved equally by a Committee of the American Bar Association and a Committee of Publishers and Associations.

In no way is it legal to reproduce, duplicate, or transmit any part of this document in either electronic means or in printed format. Recording of this publication is strictly prohibited and any storage of this document is not allowed unless with written permission from the publisher. All rights reserved.

The information provided herein is stated to be truthful and consistent, in that any liability, in terms of inattention or otherwise, by any usage or abuse of any policies, processes, or directions contained within is the solitary and utter responsibility of the recipient reader. Under no circumstances will any legal responsibility or blame be held against the publisher for any reparation, damages, or monetary loss due to the information herein, either directly or indirectly.

Respective authors own all copyrights not held by the publisher.

The information herein is offered for informational purposes solely, and is universal as so. The presentation of the information is without contract or any type of guarantee assurance.

The trademarks that are used are without any consent, and the publication of the trademark is without permission or backing by the trademark owner. All trademarks and brands within this book are for clarifying purposes only and are the owned by the owners themselves, not affiliated with this document.

Chapter 1: Reiki as a Complimentary and Alternative Medicine

Reiki is a non-invasive curative method that endorses relaxation, improves the natural remedial abilities of the human body, and nurtures emotional, mental and mystical well-being. Reiki exists based upon the awareness of a power field that infuses the body of every human being.

Reiki tries to reinstate order towards the physique whose life force or energy became unbalanced. The therapeutic energy of Reiki could be applied to deliver relief from illnesses, like fatigue, aches, anxiety, adverse side outcomes of cures and medicines, joint difficulties, and similar ailments.

Reiki, being a complementary and alternative medicine, does not aim to replace, but instead is simply integrated through, any medicinal treatment, besides other treatments, to help in triggering the inner health-giving potential of the body. Reiki presently is used within a rising number of infirmaries, clinics and hospitals throughout the world.

In a Reiki sitting, the person getting Reiki stays fully dressed and rests on a comfy table whereas the Reiki expert lightly puts his hands within various places on the physique of the patient. The patient usually feels relaxed and peaceful during the one hour session.

Shorter therapies can also be provided to someone on a hospice chair, bed or lounger. Do take note that Reiki is not an organization of spiritual beliefs, but instead simply a calming treatment where natural soothing vibrations exist transmitted by the palms of a Reiki expert, who is acting by way of a channel, to the physique of the receiver.

Reiki is currently so popular that it is even offered at the famous Mayo Clinic as nearly 40% of grown-up patients had reported using complementary and alternative medicine or CAM. Doctors embracing these therapies often combine them by mainstream therapeutic rehabilitations spawning the innovative term, integrative medicine.

Moreover, some CAM doctors believe an imperceptible energy power flows within the body in a way that, when this life force flow becomes unbalanced or blocked, the person can turn ill. Different civilizations call this power by unlike names, like prana or chi.

Finally, the ability towards learning Reiki remains not reliant on brain capacity or ability to reflect. It also does not need years of learning and practice. It can be merely transferred from a teacher toward the apprentice. And when this occurs, one possesses and could do Reiki.

Chapter 2: The Bequests of Reiki

Reiki remains an unadulterated form of curing not reliant on personal or acquired talent or ability as previously mentioned. Thus, it is easy for anyone to learn it. Also, the character of the homeopath is less probable to affect the meaning of the Reiki experience.

The reason of a Reiki therapy is usually to lessen pain and stress, induce calmness, release emotive blockages, hurry natural mending, balance delicate energies of the body and reinforce other medicinal modalities counting traditional treatments.

Reiki functions on unalike levels the bodily, mental, expressive and divine enhancing all in the life of an individual. Reiki exists, not solely one of the ancient healing schemes in practice, but is likewise one of the highly versatile. This early Japanese technique of restoring to health uses power to equalize the physique and brain, and its advantages can stay felt in both Reiki experts and their patients.

In truth, Reiki remains believed towards improving just around any facet of existence, from bodily health, emotional wellness to reduction of stress and cerebral clarity. Reiki methods are applied to cure the physique, mind, besides the soul or spirit.

It had been established that Reiki could help folks suffering from numerous major, as well as minor, ailments. Aside from being often utilized as a CAM in hospitals nowadays, it enhances the care received by sick people from patient health support providers.

Reiki had not merely helped sick people with their physical illnesses, but similarly helped those having minor mental problems, too. Among the utmost Reiki curing health advantages is reduction of stress and rest, which activates the natural curing abilities through the immune system of the body, aids with better sleeping pattern, and develops and sustains health.

Reiki assists generate inner tranquility and concord. It could be a valuable devise in the pursuit for psychic growth and the balancing of the thoughts and sentiments. Regular Reiki therapies can make a quieter and additional peaceful condition of life, wherein an individual is well able coping with daily stress.

This cerebral balance likewise enhances studying, memory, as well as mental clearness. Reiki could heal mental and emotional injuries, work over dysfunction, and in more harsh situations, can aid alleviate abrupt changes of temper, fear, irritation and anger.

Reiki could also fortify and settle personal relations because Reiki improves your competence to appreciate and love. It can expose you to the persons around you, besides helping your affairs grow. By cultivating your ability for understanding, Reiki lets you connect through people at a profounder level.

Courtesy of: https://www.google.com.ph/search?q=free+images+on+Reiki

Reiki presents relief throughout emotional suffering and grieving process. It cleanses and frees the sentiments, preventing them from becoming so drained and proposes perspective. On the bodily level, it helps towards relieving pain from, to name a few, migraine, sciatica or arthritis.

It similarly helps in conjunction with chronic pain, warning signs of insomnia, anxiety, asthma, depression, menopausal indications, addiction and chronic exhaustion. Reiki accelerates recovery from surgical procedures or lasting illnesses.

As it facilitates in regulating traditional medicine and treatment, it likewise has the tendency to lessen side effects. Reiki could be a real way towards treating immediate difficulties, like mental or physical illness. By assisting to sustain a condition of bodily and emotive balance, Reiki could not just treat complications, but maybe even stop them from developing.

Therefore, Reiki remains for everybody as it cures adults, children, toddlers, babies, people of advanced years and household pets. It can complement your yoga practice by offering balance, strength, and creativity. But to know that you stand ready to receive the gifts of Reiki, here are the signs:

1.   You value yourself and all life forms.

You own a readiness to cure yourself from the inside, and a wish to enlarge this transformation to the whole world. You stay motivated towards helping the earth become a healthier place this day and age until the years to come.

2. You trust alternative curing.

Conventional treatment serves a vital purpose, yet you similarly accept whatever is yonder tradition. You love yoga, massage, acupuncture, as well as other relaxation techniques.

3. You welcome unexplained moments.

Maybe you could sense the energy of another person when they saunter into an area, or sense a prickly sensation whenever you touch a quartz gem. You may even see the hues in the aura of a human being and recognize these as bequests that could be explored more instead of feared.

4. You possess faith in the presence of something grander.

Reiki literally denotes universally-guided energy, and its practitioners exist as vehicles holding faith within the procedure, though they could not always perceive it through their eyesight. You respect an advanced power, somewhat loving, besides larger compared to you, however you select to call this Being.

5. You stand ready aimed at your being to transform.

With Reiki attunement, doors open for the rest of your lifetime and what you on no occasion thought probable once begins working using the energy brought forth by Reiki. What does not serve you would gradually leave your existence, and fresh opportunities would enter.

Chapter 3: The Reiki Principles and Affirmations

Like each system that deals with power, Reiki experts are so conscious of the affirmative and adverse energies swirling around them. The mission of their life is towards eradicating negative forces and harnessing positive powers for the improvement of their selves, patients, besides the human race in general.

So, Reiki experts attach great importance towards building up character among Reiki followers. Everyone is provided five assertions that must be a part of his daily life. Surprisingly, these affirmations taught to Reiki learners were not decreed by Dr. Usui, the creator of Reiki.

These principles were advocated by the Japanese Meiji monarch as the five directing spiritual philosophies for the people of Japan. Dr. Usui accepted them as they assisted Reiki apprentices build better awareness within their day-to-day practice. These Reiki principles start through words signifying as only aimed at the present day:

...I will be grateful.

Be thankful from your heart inward as inner intention remains the central element within this belief. Simple stuffs as saying thanks or a few kind words, forgiving, smiling, and having a grateful heart can advance the life of others and enable them to be happy.

Moreover, being thankful conveys joy in the spirit. This exists as the number one affirmation that directs the focus of the learner towards the necessity to continuously count his benedictions instead of bemoaning all that he does not have in his life.

This awareness brings within it a sense of contentment in living and builds a real environment of plenty. It attaches the person to the riches that stay buried within the realization and nurtures a feeling of marvel. It creates the Reiki practitioner modest, stabilizes, as well as calms his thoughts, and supports his resolution in facing adversities.

A noble way towards beginning is maintaining a grateful attitude while performing Reiki on other people. This averts the ego from affirming itself as every session stays regarded by way of a chance to do service. Also, every action is seen by way of an opportunity to release an obligation for the abundance that Mother Nature has bestowed on everyone. One starts to perceive the prosperity bestowed resulting to the geometric growth of a grateful heart.

...I will not worry.

While resentment deals by past, as well as present proceedings, worry handles future concerns. Although apprehension is sometimes a bad phenomenon, endless doubts may pack the mind of a person where each bores a little hole within the soul and body. While ire requires an intensive Reiki therapy to eradicate obstacles, anxiety requires the power to exist spread all over the whole body.

Releasing worry nurses back to health the body. This exists as the number two affirmation as worry is a manifestation of a dread on desires being not realized. It remains also a sign that the sense of self is prevalent and would not tolerate any loss of face.

Worry can impact the entire being and deprive the person of rest and appetite, distort facial countenance and cause a great deal of pressure to him, besides those surrounding him. Worry is a statement of a trust deficiency in the universe. When at hand is a vow to let go of worry from your thoughts, you stand taking the first stage towards enablement.

It stays as a demand to perform your responsibility without anticipation on the yields of your act. It exist as a condition of thoughts where you would take proper and correct action aimed at an agreed task, but would not concentrate on the outcomes of the undertaking.

You would develop a calm state of thoughts where the act, not the consequences, is essential. This is a position of attention where you would trust the universe to decide upon what stays best and highly appropriate to attain the result of a specified action.

This would help you perceive the little hindrances of life as tests posed towards you through the universe. It would remove your stress and abet you to develop a neutral perspective upon the occurrences that transpire in your existence. You would appreciate that unease for the occasions is all right, but should not cause you to be anxious.

...I will not be angry.

Anger aimed at the own self, other people or the world in general, creates grave blockages within energy. Thus, anger is considered as the utmost complex internal enemy. Reiki exists as an outstanding tool towards removing obstructions caused by anger, which accumulated within the physique over the years.

As Reiki cannot eliminate the excess current fury occurring during the present day, hence, there is need for this affirmation. After all, letting go of rage brings peace into the mind. This exists as the number three of the affirmations where anger is a job of the self and should be known in that manner.

A disgruntled ego responds with wrath and resistance towards anger would make it tenacious. Therefore, it needs to come about eradicated. This confirmation is a communication of your wish to get rid of the fury and, eventually, the sense of self. When antagonism rises in you, take a breather and inspect it impassively. Reiki experts advocate that whenever anger arise within you, it will be best to imagine it by way of a bloodshot fiery sphere that you fling away from yourself, or slowly expanding until it exists completely driven away.

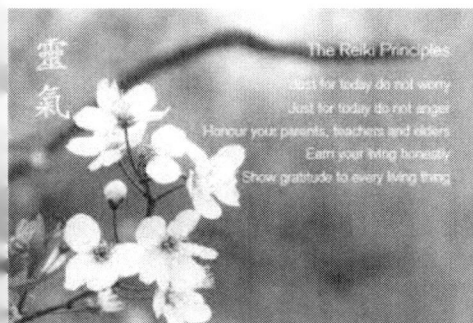

The Reiki Principles
Just for today do not worry
Just for today do not anger
Honour your parents, teachers and elders
Earn your living honestly
Show gratitude to every living thing

Courtesy of:
https://www.google.com.ph/search?q=free+images+on+reiki+principles

...I will do my work honestly.

This belief calls for everyone to support themselves and their family decently without causing harm on others. Earning an upright living is having an honorable existence and working honestly brings abundance in the soul. This pronouncement stays a usual corollary towards the previous affirmations.

Honesty remains a readiness to admit limitations, as well as work on strengths towards the finest of existing abilities. This avowal re-establishes your interaction with the true you, besides enabling you to transcend the sense of self, which attempts to outwit and exists dishonest of abilities owned.

It would bring by it a profound contentment, as well as acceptance, of your own self being as you exist. This would be mirrored in your approach to existence and lend you a hand to live your lifetime with thankfulness and open-mindedness of the weaknesses of other people.

This consciousness will abolish your exasperation and astound your inclination to be concerned about aftermaths that you bragged about deceitfully. Finally, the last of the declarations is a festivity of existence itself:

...I will be kind to every living thing.

This principle requires everyone to honor their parents, teachers and elders as kindness brings love in the mind. This announcement is envisioned to nurture in the practitioner of Reiki the wisdom of unity with every living thing on the planet, as well as the entire universe. It exists as a principle that Christ supported in the Holy Bible asking all to love their neighbor in the same manner they love themselves.

It exists also a request to humanity to do to other people what he would wish to be done to him. By confirming that you would spend the time giving, besides spreading affection, you live delving in the origins of life itself. Consequently, you stand defining the connotation of existence and creation.

As a practitioner of Reiki, you acknowledge that a Supreme Being created this universe for love. He wants to give out His love, as well as wants to stay loved. Love exists as the groundwork upon which the totality of the universe is defined and in its absence, life perishes.

Hate stands an invite to death and sin while Reiki endures as an affirmative energy given out of love. It survives a soothing and healing energy that bears affection to the person it holds coursing out of. You, as the channel of diffusion, must become an epitome of the adoration.

You also must live as an actual instrument transmitting the power unconditionally and selflessly. Reiki verifications are beyond the private Reiki domain. They coexist as universal supports that stand as the precise foundations of each spiritual philosophy.

A person who severely follows these five creeds of the Reiki teaching would find that he becomes directly linked to the source of power, and the further he shares, the additional he obtains to share. Furthermore, following the five tenets of Reiki will surely assist anyone to manage stress in his day-to-day living.

Chapter 4: The Reiki Symbols

These stay bequeathed from a master to another master and remained used aimed at attuning additional initiates in the Reiki linage. More importantly though, these symbols are employed for protection and healing, are ways of directing attention to properly connect to specific healing linkages and boosts up the power of Reiki.

Cho Ku Rei – Power symbol

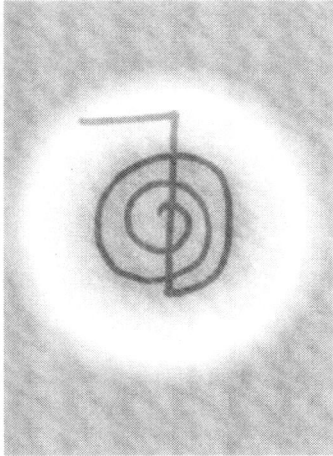

Courtesy of: https://www.google.com.ph/search?q=free+images+of+Reiki+power+symbol

The main use of this symbol is towards increasing Reiki force, drawing energy from everywhere of you, besides focusing it wherever you wish to. Make this sign above the patient or your own self and silently say the line, "Cho Ku Rei" three times.

If you want to employ the representation to transport energy to your own self, turn it around. It exists as an all-purpose sign and can stay used aimed at anything, anyplace:
1. For instant treatments;
2. In rooms of patients or hospitals;
3. On diet, water, pills and herbs;
4. Spiritual defense;
5. To assist manifestation;
6. To cleanse negative forces;
7. To sanction other symbols of Reiki; and,
8. To lid energies subsequent to treatment.

Sei Hei Ki – Mental or Emotional symbol

Courtesy of:
https://www.google.com.ph/search?q=free+images+of+Reiki+mental/emotional+symbol

It stands used chiefly for mental and emotional curing, restores harmony and emotive balance, and relaxes the thoughts. It is very worthy for:

1. Aid in removing habits;
2. Cleansing;
3. Clears emotive blockages to align the higher chakras, energy hubs within the human body;
4. For treating past sufferings;
5. In reflections to trigger Kundalini, a force that lives in the body of everyone, usually within an inactive state;
6. Psychic defense;
7. Remove bad feelings and undesirable energies; and,
8. To equalize both sides of the brain.

Hon Sha Ze Sho Nen – Distant healing symbol

Courtesy of:
https://www.google.com.ph/search?q=free+images+of+the+reiki+distant+healing+symbol

This is employed to transmit Reiki across time and distance to anybody and everything. It stays also sketched when transporting a remote attunement.

Tam-A-Ra-Sha – Balancing symbol

Courtesy of:
https://www.google.com.ph/search?q=free+images+of+reiki+balancing+symbol

This balancing and unblocking symbol is used to:
1. Ground and balance energy;
2. Helps toward unblocking the power chakra centers allowing it to move; and,
3. If drawn over a painful area, it helps reducing or dissipating the pain felt.

Dai Ko Myo – Master symbol

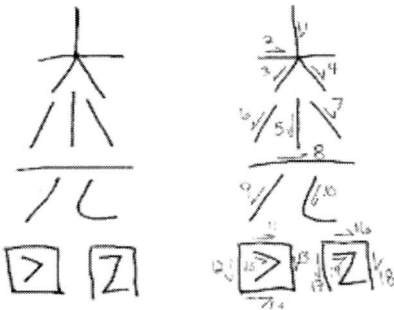

Usui (or Traditional) Dai Ko Myo

Courtesy of:
https://www.google.com.ph/search?q=reiki+master+symbol+dai+ko+myo

It exists as the highly powerful character in the group of Reiki symbols as it can only be utilized by Reiki masters. This figure is employed to cure the spirit. Since it manages the spirit and the unworldly nature, consequently, it corrects diseases at the fundamental source within the aura or energy fields.

It facilitates providing peace and enlightenment, as well as allows the person to become additionally psychic and intuitive. With exercise, this mark brings deep life modifications.

Symbols can become activated within any of these ways:
1. By finger-drawing them or with through the third eye;
2. By imagining them;
3. By saying the name of the symbol three times; or,

4. By sketching them on the center of the palm;

In activating these symbols, what matters most is the intention. Also, during healing, apply these symbols first on your individual hands or palms and draw them again or visualize the exact symbols upon the crown chakra of the patient, the places for treatment, and the hand or palm of the person being treated.

If you cannot recall the Reiki icon, use the name of the symbol because they have equal power. With constant practice, the images will turn out to be less significant as the emphasis will shift to the intention of the particular energies needed.

Courtesy of:
https://www.google.com.ph/search?q=free+images+of+reiki+symbols

Chapter 5: The Reiki Chakras

To comprehend Reiki and the palm positions employed, one must have even just rough information of the chakras. The hand placements used in America covers, besides treats, all the main chakras, being connected both to the body organs and the unique layers within the force.

Chakra exists as a Sanskrit term referring to a wheel that rotates around its personal axis, as well as can turn slow or fast. A chakra would spin depending on the level of energy within your structure. These chakras exist in all human beings.

As we all have a body, we likewise have a subtle body and chakras represent the parts of a vast network of subtle energies. We all know that live cells from people, animals, besides plants, emit invisible powers. Simple clusters of live tissue give out aura or a kind of glow that could be grasped on a Kirlian photograph.

Specialized collection of cells making up the physical body parts creates extra organized power patterns. The system of the human body consists of secretion, sensory, reproduction, breathing, digestion and circulation. Correspondingly, there, too, are six chakras aimed at each bodily function.

The mind and the entire being likewise have a chakra, building a sum of seven major chakras. These chakras stay situated atop the navel, head, solar plexus, forehead, heart, throat, and in the far end of the pelvis. Every chakra holds a counterpart organ within the physical structure:

The *root chakra* fits together by the rectum and large intestine, and also holds a definite influence upon the role of the kidneys.

The *navel chakra* goes to the system involved with reproduction, the ovaries and testicles, and likewise the urinary bladder.

The *solar plexus chakra* exists in relation towards the small intestine, liver, spleen, gall bladder and stomach.

The *heart chakra* fit in to the arms and heart.

The *throat chakra* relays to the throat and lungs.

The *third eye or forehead chakra* has its place with the mind, face, eyes, nose and all other senses.

The *crown chakra* is not limited to any organ, but relates to the total being.

Hence, there is a strong connection amid the state of the organ and its corresponding chakra. A chakra could be overly active, inactive or within balance. Using Reiki could give the chakras equilibrium and the body organs good health.

Chapter 6: The Reiki Hand Positions for

Self-Healing

Intention to cure is as simple as putting your palms on your own self or anyone else, and permitting Reiki towards flowing. Many folks, however, feel the situation necessitates asking Reiki towards flowing when beginning a session. This humble practice of requesting Reiki towards flowing will result to a reverence for Reiki, the individual receiving the power and your own self as the channel.

Method 1

At the start of a Reiki session, you might wish bringing your palms into the "Namaste" pose at the chest and bowing gently. Namaste transpires spoken by a small bow besides the palms pressed to each other, and the fingers aimed upwards with the thumbs near to the torso. Then, silently ask Reiki to flow into, as well as through you.

Method 2

You may also raise your palms up over your head in the onset of a Reiki sitting and picture the Reiki running down from the heaven into your palms, in and throughout you flowing.

Moreover, surrender is the first key of Reiki, which means simply allowing Reiki towards flowing in, as well as through you, and direct you with the recipient of the Reiki therapy in the finest healing. Remain attentive and conscious as you submit to the stream of the Reiki healing energy.

Giving your own self-healing is an extremely important Reiki facet. It is very highly recommended that you execute self-healing regularly, if possible daily as a beginner. Aside from improving your well-being, it would balance, as well as center, your mind, body and spirit structure, thereby permitting for an intensely increased stream of Reiki power during the healing sittings.

Most prominently, it would definitely upsurge your internal guidance, assisting you towards piloting everyday circumstances more positively, and delivering guidance aimed at your development when proper. The rudimentary self-treatment hand placements are like this:

Hands meeting on the topmost part of the skull;

One palm on the temple while the other palm on the rear of the skull midway amid the base and the crown;

Hands lying above the eyes;

Hands covering the ears;

One palm on the higher chest while the other atop the solar plexus where the ribs meet; and,

Hands upon the area of the hips.

Relax within each pose for five minutes before shifting position. Practice these placements until they become familiar while you gain confidence. Gradually allow your palms to be directed by your instinct. As you exercise and hold a bit of patience, you would gain familiarity and commence trusting your internal guidance.

You could not really commit an error as your healing meetings are continually watched by the Supreme Being to safeguard that your hard work will constantly be compensated. Begin a treatment to yourself with similar reverence and respect you have when providing Reiki on others.

Chapter 7: Reiki and Stress Reduction

Reiki exists as a calming light feel therapy that helps the cognizance and physique in restoring to its innate state of equilibrium. Clinical study and certain preliminary proofs from a few studies prove that Reiki therapy can become beneficial aimed at:

1. Depression and anxiety;

2. Improved rate variables of heart patients;

3. Insomnia;

4. Issues on digestion;

5. Overall wellbeing;

6. Pain, discomfort, besides other soothing care

7. Recovery from sports injury or surgery;

8. Side results from treatment of cancer, including biliousness and exhaustion; and,

9. Stress relief.

The final benefits linked with Reiki therapy are towards feeling healthier, happier, as well as progression to a condition of better self-awareness. These ideas are comparable to related forms of medicine originating from the East and mind and body exercises, including shiatsu, meditation, Traditional Chinese Medicine, Tai Chi, acupuncture, Qi Gong and yoga.

Reiki remains very simple to study as an exercise for caring and balancing the self. Self-treatment stays especially supportive for folks undergoing therapy for medical issues, or who endures chronic fitness conditions. Reiki therapy is a helpful tool uses as a supplement to orthodox medicine.

Through Reiki, you learn to face stress positively. Interestingly, pressures are needed aimed at survival. Stressful states stimulate originality and knowledge. Unfortunately though, stress overpowers many people throwing their nervous systems off balance.

This stands where calming techniques are needed, and not only do they convey your return to the state of equilibrium, but it similarly puts you within a sharp condition of willingness. Thinking positively is a psychological attitude allowing thoughts, terms and imageries that stay beneficial towards growth and victory, into your thoughts and life.

An affirmative mind, as embodied in the Reiki affirmations, anticipates contentment, joy, well-being and a fruitful outcome of each action and situation. So, whatsoever the thoughts expect, it finds. If you anticipate favorable and good results, and undertake the needed actions ensuring your achievement, you would, more frequently than not, attain it.

Positive thoughts bring internal tranquility, success, better relationships, enhanced health, contentment and fulfillment. It equally helps the everyday affairs of existence move smoothly, besides making life appear promising and bright.

And positive thoughts are contagious. People surrounding you collect on your dispositions and stay affected as a result. Therefore, think about contentment, good well-being and accomplishment and you would cause persons to love you, as well as desire helping you since they like the aura that an affirmative mind produces.

Chapter 8: Reiki Meditation

Reiki exists as a delightful relaxation method and healing power workout. If you happen to be a practitioner of Reiki, you know that whenever Reiki therapy is performed for the self, it transpires like introspection by itself. So, place your palms on your physique for some minutes, letting the universal life force energy flowing through your palms to your entire body.

Take moments to calm down and go profoundly into an incredible meditative condition. Usually, a practitioner puts his hands upon the recipient over the chakras, at work along the rear and front of the physique. Bear in mind that all chakras, major and minor alike, on the body are all acupressure contacts of the energy cores. To try:

Step 1:

Lie down or sit comfortably making sure your backbone is straight. Take a couple of deep inhalations imaging that the greatest pure affectionate and curing energy starts entering your physique. When you breathe out, imagine that each tension, the entire negativities, ache, anger, vexation and depression are running away from your physique together with your breathing out. Let them flow out of you completely.

Step 2:

Place your palms on every major chakra in front of your physique and retain them above each one for around three minutes, unless your physique requires them to stay a little longer. It stays an impeccable opportunity at this moment to move in line with your physique.

Hence, listen to your body and have faith. As you keep your palms over your chakras, envisage the life power energy from the whole universe inflowing to your physique and feeling it through your palms to the remaining parts of your body aimed at the utmost good of every body part. Savor the deep serenity and vitality within your whole body.

Step 3:

Place both your hands amid fingers altogether over the topmost part of your crown. Hold, besides listening, to your physique gently in the midst of loving care. Inhale and exhale nicely, gradually and profoundly while focusing on optimistic qualities and unleashing rejections to relax further.

Step 4:

Very mildly, take your palms and put them upon your brow covering your eyes, if you find them comfortable. Hold while relaxing.

Step 5:

Gently shift your palms to the rear of your skull. Find the place there that is highly comfortable and maintain your palms there.

Step 6:

Next, put your palms very lightly on your throat not pushing too greatly as needed to continue breathing and feeling comfortable. You may put equally your hands upon the frontage of your throat, or one in front, while the other on the rear of the neck. Find a place that works best for you to hold in a relaxing way.

Step 7:

Now, place your palms over your shoulders in the rear with fingers aimed down. Then, hold and rest.

Step 8:

Place your palms now upon your torso very softly to cover your heart. Hold, listen, and then relax.

Step 9:

Now, slightly move your palms to the lower part of your chest close the lowermost ribs, hold and calm down.

Step 10:

Place your palms over your tummy, hold and loosen up.

Step 11:

Next, shift your hands gently placing your palms above your lower abdomen touching fairly over the pubic bone. Hold, as well as relax.

Step 12:

Gently put your palms on the right and left sides of your hips, then hold and continue relaxing.

Step 13:

Move your palms and put them on every knee, hold and chill out.

Step 14:

Next, place your palms on both of your feet, covering either bottom or top as what may be more comfy for you. Hold, relax and only do this if you find this position comfortable.

Step 15:

Now, take your palms together, or just one palm, at a position of prayer and sustain it for around three minutes inhaling and exhaling naturally, besides feeling the power moving over your entire body. Feel every bit of pessimism being flushed off your being and substituted with affection, healing, as well as joy.

Conclusion

Thank you again for downloading this book!

I hope this book was able to help you to understand Reiki and its important role in reducing stress.

The next step is to follow the steps and tips cited in the book. Always remember that stress is a predictable part of living. You may be a licensed professional struggling to meet your work timeline, university student completing a requirement, or an elderly watching the days pass by, pressures or stress approach at every bend and curve.

It will always remain your choice to spend each day overcoming stress naturally or with much effort. Practicing Reiki as a relaxation technique can rally round to improve your attitude, lift your vitality and help you deal with unexpected events with calmness. Whichever way, may you permanently be supported with love, peace and happiness.

Finally, if you enjoyed this book, then I'd like to ask you for a favor, would you be kind enough to leave a review for this book on Amazon? It'd be greatly appreciated!

Click here to leave a review for this book on Amazon!

Thank you and good luck!